Like a Girl

Book 2
Astronaut

Ask your parents' permission before reading this book.

The following book features descriptions of actions performed by a professional astronaut.
Do not attempt to re-create or re-enact any plot or activity performed in this book.

Enjoy the book and stay safe!
Ashley the astronaut

I'M ASHLEY THE ASTRONAUT

Have you ever wondered what happens when you go very high into the sky?

Higher than the highest mountain, higher than airplanes, way above the clouds, is where space is.

In fact, to be in space, you have to leave planet Earth completely.

This is the International Space Station. It's where I work and live, along with my other friends: astronauts from all over the world.

But I was still curious about the sky and the stars. So I studied even more and became an expert on space.

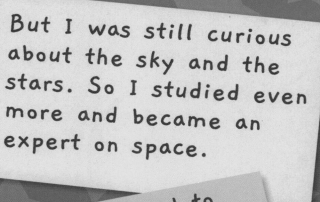

Then I wanted to learn things about the world that nobody knows yet

AND I DECIDED TO BE AN ASTRONAUT!

WOW!
The stars look so bright from here!
AND LOOK AT THE EARTH!
SO BEAUTIFUL!

I'm getting a signal from the Space Station that they're ready for my arrival.

My space suit is thick and sturdy. It protects me from the cold.

IT ALSO HAS THICK GLOVES

BOOTS

AND A HELMET

They are all attached to the suit.
I have to be completely covered to stay safe.

WOULD YOU LIKE TO SEE HOW WE SLEEP IN SPACE?
GOOD NIGHT!
Because there's no up and down, it doesn't matter which way our sleeping bags are turned.
But we do attach them to the wall, because we don't want to float around the room while we sleep.

Every day we look at Earth from our window and think about all the people we love and miss.

It looks so beautiful from up here. We all count the days until we go back.

IF YOU ARE SMART
AND STRONG
AND BRAVE
AND DREAM OF THE STARS
MAYBE YOU CAN BE AN ASTRONAUT TOO!

THE
END

NEXT
BOOK:
DOCTOR

LIKE A GIRL

A show and
tell scrapbook
adventure!

DOCTOR

BY APRIL PETER AND DANIEL SHNEOR

NEWS & UPDATES

For special insider access to future releases, promotions and more, please follow the link below and subscribe to our newsletter.

www.light-sleepers.com/subscribe

If you enjoyed this book, please consider taking a minute to write an honest review on Amazon.

Reviews are the lifeblood of indie authors and your contribution would be greatly appreciated.

Best regards,
April & Daniel

MORE BOOKS BY THE AUTHORS:

Books are available on Amazon.com

MORE BOOKS BY THE AUTHORS:

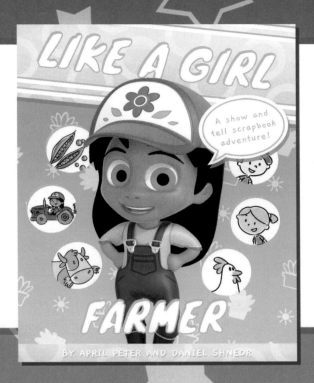

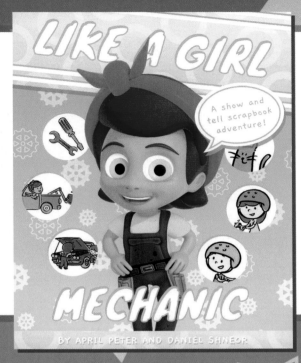

Books are available on Amazon.com

MORE BOOKS BY THE AUTHORS:

Books are available on Amazon.com

MORE BOOKS BY THE AUTHORS:

Ann Can't Sleep

By April Peter

MEG & ROB'S
WITCH TRICKS

THE WICKED STEW

DANIEL SHNEOR & APRIL PETER

MEG & ROB'S
WITCH TRICKS

NO WIN WITH A TWIN

DANIEL SHNEOR & APRIL PETER

Books are available on Amazon.com

CUT OUT AND PLAY

A printable version of this page is also available on
www.light-sleepers.com/free/

CUT OUT AND PLAY

A printable version of this page is also available on
www.light-sleepers.com/free/

CUT OUT AND PLAY

A printable version of this page is also available on
www.light-sleepers.com/free/

Made in the USA
Columbia, SC
17 June 2020